Harun Güngör - Abrurrahman Küçük

The Sources of the National Integrity:

Remainings From Asia to Anatolia

Transladet by:

Pınar Gedikoğlu

Atatürk Culture Centre Publications

ATATÜRK SUPREME COUNCIL
ATATÜRK CULTURE CENTER

Harun Güngör-Abdurrahman Küçük

The Sources of the National Integrity:
Remainings From Asia to Anatolia

Transladet by:
Pınar Gedikoğlu

Atatürk Supreme Council
Atatürk Culture Center Publication:223
Gleaning from Turkish Culture: 61

Harun Güngör-Abdurrahman Küçük
The Sources of the National Integrity:
Remainings From Asia to Anatolia
©Atatürk Culture Center, 2000

ISBN: 975-16-1327-2
İLESAM: 2000.06.Y.0143-217

Transladet by:
Pınar Gedikoğlu

Cover & Page Design
Düş Atelyesi
+90 312 418 79 03

Printing
Düş Atelyesi

Atatürk Culture Center
G. M. K. Bulvarı 133, 06570 Maltepe-Ankara
Tel: +90 (312) 231 23 48 - 232 22 57
Fax: +90 (312) 232 43 21

PROLOGUE

It has been over 900 years since Turks come to Anatolia. Then they migrated on to the Balkans, an event that occurred more than 700 years ago. Cultures, civilizations, armies and states had their ups and downs just as the ebb and flow. At the beginning of the 20th century, they had to remain within the bounds associated with their cultural geography Nevertheless they established a free, independent and democratic republic within those boundaries. Establishing a state is not as intrinsically important in itself as protecting it and keeping it alive.

Ataturk said: "The Turkish Republic has been established on Turkish heroism and Turkish culture" The basis for Turkish heroism and Turkish culture lies in the common awareness of our integrity and security. In societies where there is no common awareness, a social-cultural structure can not be seen.

As the Atatürk Cultural Center, we are honored to undertake the duty of replying on a scientific basis to every open or covered threat or danger to our integrity and security, in line with the wishes of the honorary chairman of our institution, Atatürk. We have thus decided to present the views and opinions of scientists, to readers in booklet that would not scare them off because of their volume.

It is evident that Turkey, which has maintained its integrity, security and social peace, will constitute a deterrent for its foes and encourage the continuation of the friendship shown by its allies. During the War of Independence and its aftermate, there was no discard to speak about the politicians, thinkers and the people despite of great economic difficulties suffered. Following 1938 discord began to be observed.

We have turned into a society over sensitive to damaging effects, open to mischief and its integrity some what disrupted; we have to overcome these faults and make self-confidence and internal balance awareness of the basis for a sound growth. We do not have an axe to grind with anybody and we do not want anyone to pick a bone with us. However to achieve this aim, first we have to establish unity and integrity.

National security and national integrity are important concepts, which should always be taken into consideration for the survival of the Turkish Republic. In countiers where concepts are not clean anomie of ideas can be seen. Anomie (Social instability) is a negativity, which obstructs the continuation of societies in history. Everyone should read the "Tenth Anniversary speech" delivered by Atatürk (on the tenth anniversary of the Republic) to reconsider their duty and do whatever befalls them in order to give the concepts a national outlook and to clarify these targets.

The idea which forms the basis for the view paints expressed in this series are national interpretations which can be of help in the solution of various current problems. We would like this awareness of duty to continue and be happy by performing what befalls us.

I would like to express my thanks to İmran Baba and İbrahim Baştuğ who have been helpful in publishing these series.

Prof.Dr.Sadık Tural.

THE SİGNS OF SHAMANİSM İN THE TURKİSH (SHİİTE-BEKTASH) BELİEFS

Before discussing the relation between Bektashi beliefs and shamanism, which is still a matter of argument whether it is a religion or not, I would like to give a brief defination of Shamanism. Then I want to show the similarities between Bektashi and Sunni motives with Shamanism.

According to Eliade, Shamanism is both mystic and magic. In greater sense it is a kind of religion of archaic ecstacy techniques.[1] However according to Cauliano; it is the collection of ecstasic and trapotik methods which provides the support of spirits during the management of the relations between the clans of spirits, humanities and the social sciences parallel to human world rather than a religious system.[2] The basic factor which seperates Shamanism, which comes across us as animism, animalism or

[1] Mircea Eliade, *Le Chamanisme et les techniques Archaniques del' Extase*, Payot, Paris, p. 14.

[2] Mircea Eliade, Ioan P. Couliano, *Dictionnaire des religions*, Paris 1990, p. 99.

zoomorfism, from other religions and beliefs is the close relation between the ones living in Shamanism and the ancestors. In Shamanism this relation is being formed by the magician, sorcerers, physicians and the religious functionaries, which are known as Shamans. It is quite wrong to define the old Turkish religion as Shamanism as its dimensions exceeds Shamanism. Along with this, Shamanism and the old Turkish religion had many similarities and in this respect we can say that Shamanism can just be a dimension of the old Turkish religion. The moderate and vulnarable structure of Shamanism caused this religion to end and was replaced by other official religions. We would like to compare Shamanism, which is a social truth with Bektashism. For this reason we want to give a brief explanations of some Shaman tales.

1- The Rescuer Shaman Girl

In the past extraword, during the time when we were Yakut there lived a Shaman named Yölken Bıraayı. It was said that this Shaman, who was the ancestor of the Oltek community was a murderer. He use to kill the Shamans and then eat them. Bacause of this reason other Shamans became his enemy and wanted to kill him as soon as possible.

Once the Abaases (evil Souts) of nine Shamans gathered in a place and walked towards him. Later on they quickly turned into animals such as, bear, wolf, dog and even an ox.

As they became a larger group they started to eat the Shaman.

At this stage Shaman wanted to save his life and his soul became a dreadful bird and flew upon the Lena River. The others also became birds and followed him.[3]

2- The Shaman Getting The Revenge of His Ancestors

There lived a Shaman called Adagalaah. He had to compete with other Shamans.

Once Shaman, Kısınce took the form of a big bird and flew to the mount Itık Haya. The neck of Kısınce was extremely long that he could stay in one end of the river and could easilly reach to other side to eat the grasses.[4]

3- The Shaman Swallwing A Hammer

.... the Shaman just muttered by himself and then started talking with his own soul. After this Huren

---

[3] *Saman Efsaneleri ve Söylemeleri*, (translated and arranged by Fuzuli Gözelov, Celal Mehmedov) Bakı 1993 p. 84.
[4] Memmedov, Gözelov, *ibid*, p. 64.

Oool took out his own hammer and then started swallowing it.[5]

4- The Shaman who can be at seven different places at a time

When the famous Shaman to cut Kıçakan into pieces, he took the form of seven different creatures at a time. When the Shaman tried to cut one of them then Kıçakan took the form of any other Kıçakan and said "cut him into pices one more time".

When the Shaman tried to catch the other one which talked, then the third Kıçakan said "cut him into pieces one more time". This Shaman was such a kind that could be at seven different places at a time.[6]

5- The Fish Shaman

One male and one female Shaman started to compete with each other. The woman said;
"which form shall we adopt to check our powers?".

The man Shaman answered;
"lets take the form of a fish"

When the woman became a fish, she quickly dipped into the water. The man also became a fish and started

---

[5] Memmedov, Gözelov, *ibid*, p. 65.
[6] Memmedov, Gözelov, *ibid*, I p. 69.

to chase her. Within a short period of time he got her and then tried to swallowing her, but the Shaman women was a larger fish then him so she swallowed him.

After swallowing him the Shaman woman became a bird and flew back to her house.[7]

6- To bring death to the cattle

One day Küstek came to Terbeet Mikhails house as a guest. The wife of Terbeet Mikhael was very mean, Shaman asked the Woman to cook meat but she said that they did not have any meat. Even though they had it but she did not cook it.

Shaman said to the woman "just wait for a while and you will have meat" and then went out. After the Shaman left the host found out that all his cows and oxes were dead.[8]

7- The power of the Shaman woman

There was a very famous woman known as Çırtak Ool. Once Çırtak Ool was in a stranger house. When she was there she saw a glass of alcholic drink and she asked for some drink but the owner of the house said that there was no drink.

[7] Memmedov, Gözelov, *ibid*, I p 76.
[8] Gavril Vasilyeviç Ksenofontov, *Shamanizm Izbrannie Trudı*, Yakutsk 1992, p. 184.

Çırtak Ool said nothing and left the house. The next day thunderbolt fell on that house and the house burnt into ashes.[9]

8- Shaman teraring off the stars

Once upon a time, there was a Shaman called Yotuuleeh Yergen Oyun. An event about him is told: It was said that a star appeared in the village, in his time. Later on the fertillity decreased. Trees and all the plants dried. The world was faced with starvation. A freezing wind was blowing from west during winters.

The Shaman saw the state of his land and quickly flew towards the sky and went near to the one who sent that star to fight with him. As the Shaman flew to the sky, he wrapped himself with his fur made from wolf leather, tied his sharp axe to his waist. Shaman fought with him continiously seven days and seven nights. It is said that as he cut the star into pieces, some ice pieces dropped from the sky. Then one night Shaman came down from the sky and said "I plucked and cut the star into pieces, I put the world life into order". When Shaman fought, he freezed because of cold.

There is a belief that the life on the world hasn't changed since then. During that period, human generation didn't seperated from each other.[10]

---

[9] Memmedov, Gözelov, *ibid*, p. 64.
[10] Memmedov, Gözelov, *ibid*, p. 65-66.

9- The miracle of Shaman Sat Soyul

These events occured in the home country of Shaman Sat Soyul, on the shores of Terektig stream. It was an evening (sun set) in autumn. As the Shaman Sat Soyul stabed his knife to his chest and noticed that the knife made from iron, dropped from the sky and was pierced after each mallet stroke.

Knife penatrated in his chest all in all and the Shaman fell down weakly. People blieved that he was dead. However, after a while he moved, took the knife off and then started to fight quitely.[11]

10- Shaman Mahunay

Shaman Mahunay was making horses to move, before harnessing them to sledge. It was said that the chief of the Irkuts wanted to test him.

He said "Bring seventy carriage of straws and spread on the Shaman and burn them". When people heard this happenning, they carried it out. When the fire extinguished, they noticed that Shaman Mahunay stood up inside the ashes, shook off the dust on him and then went away.[12]

[11] Memmedov, Gözelov, *ibid*, p. 68.
[12] Ksenofontov, *ibid*, p. 185.

11- The Shaman walking on the water

In the early days, there was living a famous Shaman called as Kaçikaat Oyun, in the town of Kaçikat. There are several miracles told about him, he was known by his miracles. One of them was:

One day, Kaçikat came to the town of Nemyegin and asked Sokolooh, a native Shaman of the town, to set out on a journey with him. Sokdooh accepted the offer.

When they came to the shore of the River Lena, Kaçikat put on his shoes and crossed the river by walking on the river. Shaman Sokolooh called a boat from the opposite shore and anvacant boat came and stopped near him. Then Shaman Sokolooh got on the boat and crossed the river.[13]

12- Shaman Totogoş

There was a great Shaman among the Telengits. One day, the Russian Tzar ordered all the Shamans to be burnt. Only Totogoş wasn't burnt. The Russian Tzar saw the state and then called Totogoş as Abıs Kam and let him to take part in the battles.

[13] Memmedov, Gözelov, *ibid*, p. 69.

Either Pyrot Khan himself or the son of Elzen Khan had become ill. Khan called Shaman Abıs to fight for him. Abıs Karez came and saved the patient. Khan gave nine wild horses and a horse keeper to him.

Totgoş sent horses to the other shore. Then he stayed in a place near by Khan's country, secretly. The aim of Totogoş was to kidnap the daughter of the Khan. Shaman had talked to the girl and they had agreed. Shaman kidnapped the girl in the night time. Then Khan sent his cavalries and ordered "if you catch them, tie my daughter to the tail of the horses till each part of her body turns into slices and cut the head of the Shaman".

The cavalries did as they were told. They cut the girl into two parts and also chopped off Shaman's head from his body. Then they tied the seperated head to the strap of horse's sadle. However, the head started to laugh. also Shaman' body started to move and come after the cavalries. Then they brought him to Oyrot Khan. There Totogoş transformed into stone and he still stays there. To some people this stone seems yellow, to some it seems white and to some it seems red.

Now, a great Shaman lives in a place near to that stone. It is said that the Shamans who are weak die and the strong Shamans without any damage, near the stone. The religious community still sacrifices to this stone.[14]

13- Helping old man and woman to have child

Sielleh Esuryu was very old. Also his wife was very old and they hadn't had a child. One day, two Shamans visited them. They said that they came from the province of yakut and that they were Kaçikats from the North Koil. That night they stayed as a guest there. During a conversation, the hosts said that they never had a child and they got very old.

The Shamans spent the night there. In the morning one of the Shamans said: I had a dream in which I was told that you will have a child. The hosts requested the Shamans to pray to God for a child for them. Shamans said that they did such a thing before so they accepted tehir request.

Firstly, the Shamans prayed to the Ayıısıt (God of birth) to give a child to the old people. However Ayıısıt didn't help them. Then the elder Shaman said that they could pray to the God of rain and lightning, as once he helped him. The hosts begged the Shamans to pray to this God; thereupon the Shamans

[14] Memmedov, Gözelov, *ibid*, p. 63.

danced and prayed all day and night. Eventually, they were able to reach to Seyulen Bılıt Terayocer, God of the rain and lightning. This God promised to give two sons to the old man and woman in return of Shaman vows, sacrifices and prays.

The God wanted one of the childs name to be Çohuh and the others to be Syyule Bagdarın which is the sybol of the clouds and the rain.

The Shamans told the old man and woman what the God wished that they should read brr... (a kind of prayer) for the souls of the children.

The Shamans said that they would visit them after three years and then left. When they were leaving, the hosts gave many gifts to them. After three years they came back, as they promised. When they returned they saw that the old man and the woman had two sons. The hosts were given many presents again.[15]

14- The revivification of the death

In the past times, there was a Shaman called as Berges Oyun. Also at the same time there was a another Shaman called as Hamnatçıt Oyun from the Haçın nation.

---

[15] Ksenofontov, *ibid*, p. 193-194.

Bergese Oyun had a friend. One day his friends' beloved son was suffering from tuberculosis. His friend sent a man to Bergese Oyun living in Vilyuy and wanted Bergese Oyun to cure his sons' sickness. When Bergese Oyun recieved the invitation, he said to the man who brought the invitation "I'm not able to go as I am sick but there is a Shaman, called Hamnatçıt, who is as good as me. Take the child to him".

The man immediately applied to Shaman Hamnatçıt, as Bergese said. This Shaman agreed to help them. They set out for the journey. In the morning, Shaman said to the man "I'm going there for a vain. There should be five Shamans there with him. The condition of the patient might be worse and when we set there the patient might be dead and I will subjugate. You will take the seat below the horse and put it in to the centre. Then you will give me a glass of milk to drink".

They went to the house of Inahsıt. They saw that his son had just died. There were many people in the house and also the five Shaman were among them. Most of them were crying. When they saw the Shaman, they said that they made him come for vain.

Shaman Namatçık paid no attention to them and started to subjugate. Firstly, he asked the host to boil some milk.. When Shaman subjugated the death, boy returned back to life and asked for milk. He he said "either I died or I was fainted". Namçık said "I had just notified with my souls yesterday, and saved his life. So the patient didn't die but he fainted". Then the Shaman turned to the father of the patient and said that his son wouldn't die before three hundred years. Then the child's father gave three horses carrying presents for the Shaman and sent him back to his house.[16]

General evaluation

In the stories mentioned so far, which are chosen with great care, there are some extraordinary events which happened with Shamans like Kam, Oyun, Bahşi, Shaman and Belki. When we compare the miracles of the Shamans with the miracles of Baba, Eren, Alp, Alperen and Abdal seen in the Alavi -Bektashi legends, we can clearly see their influences to each other and can easily stabilize their extensions in Anatolia. Starting from this view, let's examine Shaman patterns one by one.

a) To adopt different forms (see stories no. 1, 2, 3, 4, 5)
b) to be seen in different places at the same time (story no.)
c) to give harm to the one who lies (story no. 7)

---

[16] Memmedov, Gözelov, *ibid*, p. 111 (Beside to compare see: *Menâkib-ı Hacı Bektash-ı Velî "Vilayetname"* by: Abdülbaki Gölpınarlı, İstanbul 1990, p. 18-19).

Patterns in sunni legends	Patterns in Alaouite-Bektashi legends	Patterns in shaman legends
To be seen in different dresses at the same time	To be seen in different dresses at the same time	To be seen in different dresses at the same time
To have no limit in terms of place	To have no limit in terms of place	To have no limit in terms of place
To be seen revived after death	To be seen revived after death	To be seen revived after death
To know the thoughts	To know the thoughts	To know the thoughts
To learn events from future	To learn events from future	To learn events from future
To make a death revive	To make a death revive	To make a death revive
To cure illnesses	To cure illnesses	To cure illnesses
To dominate powers of nature	To dominate powers of nature	To dominate powers of nature to pluck the star
To punish enemies in different ways	To punish enemies in different ways	To punish enemies in different ways
	To be seen like an animal	To be seen like an animal
	To fly on the sky	To fly on the sky
	Not to be burnt in the fire	Not to be burnt in the fire
To challenge another saint and to overwhelm him	To challenge another saint and to overwhelm him	To challenge another shaman and to overwhelm him
	To transform human, animal and plant into stone	To transform human into stone
	To make enemies meet with disaster and harm	To make enemies meet with disaster and harm
	To make old woman and man have a child	To make old woman and man have a child
	To across the river by splitting the water	To pass the other side by walking on the water[17]

[17] This comparison has been made by considering January's investigations, (A. Yaşar Ocak, *Türk Halk İnançlarında ve Edebiyatında Evliya Menkabeleri,* Ankara 1984, pp. 91-93

d) not to be burnt in the fire (story no. 10)
e) to transform the people in to stones (story no. 12)
f) to read one's mind (story no. 10)
g) to swallow an object (story no. 3)
h) to penetrate a sharp material into one's own body (story no. 9)
i) 0to dominate on the powers of the nature (story no. 7)
j) to challenge another Shaman and to overwhelm him (story no. 5)
k) to revive a dead person (story no. 14)
l) to walk on the water (story nno. 11)
m) to help old man and woman blessed with a child (story no. 13)

We can enumerate the similarities and the common points among the Shamanist beliefs, Alavi-Bektashi legends and even Sunni beliefs. To provide a much better understanding to the readers, we can make this comparison by simple illustration.

When we compare the patterns presented above with the patterns seen in Hacı Bektashi Veli's Vilayetname, we can easily observe that they have the same qualities except from the heroes mentioned in the stories. For example, when Hacı Bektaşi was taking the form of a pigeon[18] one of the saints was

---

[18] *Vilâyetname*, p. 18.

changing his form to a folkon.[19] Also, the secound dimension of changing form, which is common among the Anatolian beliefs, is the Djiin's changing their forms into human beings or goats etc. These are the beliefs which prevails in both of the societies.

In Epçe, which is a Sunni village of the town of Develi, a legend like the one about challenging a saint and overwhelming him is told. Once the Epçe Sultan, who was living in the town of Develi, wanted to visit the Sheikh who was living in the village of Havadan, which was also in the same town. Epçe Sultan riding a ram, flys towards the village of Havadan. The Shiekh of Havadan, knowing about the visit of the Epçe Sultan got on a rock and aimed to meet her. Both of the Saints meet at a certain point on the sky and greeted each other. The Epçe Sultan understood that the degree of the Sheikh was higher that hers as he came by getting on a rock. So in the rest of her life she respected him.

Also a legend like the one about Shaman Kiçakan, who returned back to life after death, is told by Evliya Çelebi. It is about Abdi Dede who lived in Kayseri. According to the legend, Abdi Dede also returned back to life after his death just like the Shaman Kiçakan.[20]

---

[19] *Vilâyetname, ibid*, p. 19.

[20] *Evliya Çelebi Seyahatnâmesi*, (translated to Turkish by: Zuhuri Danışman), İstanbul 1970, volume V, p. 77-78.

Some researchers want to tie Bektashi legends to the beliefs of the saints in Chritianity by establishing some similarities and parallelism between Bektashi legends and Christian saint's legends. However, even these few examples shows us how much the beliefs of Shamanism affected Anatolian beliefs of Bektashi and Sunni ones. Beliefs of Shamanism forms their source base.

In addition, these similarities also show how the Turks forgot their culture after converting to Islam. Additionally points out hastily that their culture has no value among Muslim Turks. Even these similarities show the deficiency of claim that the value of the past Turkish religion before becoming muslims lives just in Alavi-Bektashi marginal groups. However the truth of the matter is that the value lived among the public religiousness of the Sunni muslim Turks. at the same time.

Moreover, I want to call your attention to some points that are necessary to consider. These are the concepts each of which is an expression of a belief, used in the story except for the dominating patterns. These are "Itık, no. nine, contact with God by wearing wolf skin, transforming into stone and also the female Shamans". Itık or the Iduk is the most important religious concept formed in the Turkish culture. Sacred concepts are discriminated from the mundane by this concept.[21] The number nine was the holy no. that is used by northern and eastern Turks. Protection from all harm is seen among Anatolian folk beliefs. Another belief which is about the sacredness of the greywolf lives in a saying of the Turkmen Alaouites of Kayseri, which is "Stay with greywolf till doomsday". Female Shamans taking part in Shamanism is important to understand, when we think about the view of women especially in religions dominated by Semitic culture. Woman's role in Turkish culture is seen very clearly. Perhaps this belief is an archaic form of Bacyan-ı Rum in Anatolian Bektashi belief.

Laughter of the decapitated head;

"The decapitated head fought for three days
Gençosman became commander of the Martriers"

Transforming into stone has another important place among Anatolian folk beliefs.[22]

As it's expressed above, no. nine, Itık, Haya (the Holy Rock), Shamans wearing wolf skin, changing into stone and the religious people are quite important concepts. All these patterns are included in both

---

[21] Memmedov, Gözelov, *ibid*, p. 69.

[22] Saim Sakaoğlu, *Anadolu Türk Efsanelerinde Taş Kesilme Motifi ve Bu Efsanelerin Tıp Kataloğu*, Ankara 1980, p. 140; Hikmet Tanyu, *Dinler Tarihi Araştırmaları*, Ankara 1973, p. 41.

Alavi-Bektashi and Sunni beliefs. These patterns even form their bases.

Another important subject that should be mentioned is the reading some verses from the Holy Quran. Both in Sunni and in Alavi Bektashis the tradition of application to the religious people in case of a sickness for any other purpose is an enduring value. In this tradition, many religious or marginal applications of the Turkish Kams are made legal by making their religious and marginal applications similar to those of the Islamic patterrns. However this similarity is not just seen among Anatolian muslim folk. In Turks, it is nearly impossible to find these values of continuation. Really, in the Gagauzs, the Christian Turks, Ababu (old woman) can be shown as another example of such applications mentioned above.[23]

There are some beliefs and applications such as treatment of the evil eye (nazar) and practical ways to be protected;to tie the mouth of the wolf, to stop children's crying[24], to tie a course cloth to the branches of the trees was supposed to be holy[25] and even

[23] Harun Güngör, "Gaguz Inanışı ve Âdetleri ile ilgili Bazı Notlar", *Türk Dünyası Tarih Dergisi*, Mart 1994, no. 87, p. 26.

[24] B. Rintchen, "Moğol ve Kazak Etnografyasından Seçmeleri", translator: Harun Güngör, *Türk Dünyası Araştırmaları*, December 1985, no. 87, p. 225-229.

[25] Mihaly Hoppal, *Schamanen und Schamanismus*, Ausburg, Pattloch 1994, p. 162.

Albastı... etc. All these are still eccepted in today's Turkey, both in Sunni and Alavi -Bektashi communities in the same way together with the table stated above, all these shows that Shaman beliefs are not only effectivein Anatolian Alaouite-Bektashi understanding, but also in Sunni understanding.

But also it's necessary to mention that Alaouite-Bektashi beliefs have been influenced by Shamanism more than the Sunni beliefs. It is known that both Alaouite and Sunni values are affected by the Shamanism. However, in some recent studies has tried to be proved that there is an absolute relationship between Alaouitism and Mazdaism. Some researchers ignore the fact that **Mazdaism's object of worshipping fire is a material to be clean up Turkish thoughts and beliefs,** although they also claim that the real similarity between the two systems revolves around the "belief in fire".

In our opinion, to reject the relationship between Alaouitism and Alaoite effects on the Central Asian Turkish culture by denying the effects of Shamanism is not totally a right thing to support. However, It's caused by an ideological approach to the subject which is quite invalid.

Result:

Some people like C. Bender[26], E. Xemgin[27] and S. Bilgin[28] have been trying to create a cultural base for an ethnic distinction by separating the basis of Alaouite-Bektashi beliefs from Shamanism and also trying to reflect these beliefs as the Mazdaist beliefs. The books which are written by these people depend on ideological norms rather than scientific norms.

This method is totally incorrect as it has ben explained above. Shortly, the main cultural source of both the Anatolian Sunnis and the Alaouite-Bektashi is totally derived totally from Central Asian Shamanism beliefs. This source feeds the roots of both belif system.

[26] Cemşid Bender, *Kürt Tarihi ve Uygarlığı*, İstanbul 1991, p. 91-20.

[27] Etem Xemgin, *Alevîliğin Kökenindeki Mazda İnancı ve Zerdüşt Öğretisi*, İstanbul 1995, p. 225.

[28] M. SIRAÇ Bilgin, *Zararthursta (Zerdüşt) Hayatı ve Mazdaizm*, İstanbul 1995, p. 19 vd.

Turks' Religious Tolerance of Minorities in Anatolia (Armenians and Jewish Examples)

Abdurrahman Küçük

Introduction

The Turkish nation is known for its tolerance, in history and today. This tolerance is an inseparable feature of the Turkish nation. To help the needy and to be against to the evil deeds were the habits of the Turkish people.

Turks have always struggled with the nations that were superior to them. They were always helping to those that were inferior to them and who seeked help. There are many examples in which we can clearly recognize their tolerant character, before coming to Anatolia and during the period before converting to Islam. The   examples of the happenings are limited. The word "minority" is used to express the people belong to other religions, the same attitude was shown during the Ottoman period and also after the Ottoman period.

The Turks have behaved in a very tolerant way nearly to all Syriancs, Armenians and to Byzantineans. They also showed great respect to their cultural norms and also to their religion. They were always dealt kindly and justly. Among the Gregorian Christian minorities, Armenians and the Jews had a special place. In this short introductory part, these two communities with different races and cultures will be concerned in reflacting the tolerant character of the Turks. However it is also quite beneficial to reconsider other minorities such as the Christian Orthodok and the Greek Orthodox.

Turks behavior to the minorities of different religions and cultures was very kind and judical. They were totally free in practice of their own traditions and beliefs. They were also judged according to their own religion and moral norms. The peak of this tolerance was during the conquest of Constantinople which was the period of the rise of the Ottomans. Everybody was curious about the attitude of Sultan Mehmet, the conquerer towards the people of the conquered l and. The Christians were scared and were also very curious about their features. They were not sure whether they would have the security of life, property and religion. However Fatih Sultan tried to calm them by saying "Don't be afraid of my wrath as being my subject". The Orthodox Patriarchate didn't have a Patriarc so he chosed a new Patriarc and took the Pariarchate under his own protection. In addition to this, the Sultan gave many privileges that none of the Sultans anywhere else in during that time could vanture. He declared the given privileges through a "Ferman", which is an imperial edict. In the written Ferman, it was clearly mentioned that nobody would harm Patriarc and the Churches should be respected and never be changed into Mosques, also their ceremonies would be conducted in free evironment.

The same tolerance and privileges continued after the reign of Sultan Mehmet, the conquerer. Also in the reign of Sultan Süleyman and Sultan Selim II, broad opportunities and privileges were given to them in practising their religious beliefs and traditions. When Cyprus was conquered, Selim II said to the governor (beylerbeyi), Cadı (kadı) and to the Ministry of Finance wealth and security should be provided to the minorities and their lives, honour and property should be protected. Also in the imperial edict (ferman) he claimed that people from other religions and cultures in Cyprus were trusted to him by God and also that if anybody acted contrary to his decrees, he would be severly punished and his testimony wouldn't be accepted. He said that justice was his main concern. In addition to these, he also gave prosperity to the Bishopric of Greece Orthodox, their Churches and priests were protected and full freedom were gived to them. This priviladged position was sometimes used against the Turks by the Greek orthodoxs and the priests. The Greek Churches were used as a base in the seperation of the Greeks and the Byzantine Greeks.

Although to all these negative developments, Turks took the necessary measures and defended themselves. The Bishopric and the Greek Orthodox Churches havepreserved their existence in Istanbul till today.[1] This is the best example to show the limits of tolerance of the Turks towards the minorities. Following, as the Gregorian Christians Armenians and the Jews are given as an example, we find it unnecessary also to mention the Greek Orthodox. Later on, the tolerance shown to the Jews will be described using tehir own sources.

a) The religious tolerance of Turks towards the Gregorian Christian Armenians

The Byzantine Empire opposed the Turks while they were marching into Anatolia. In the Byzantine Empire, Orthodox Christians were dominant, the Armenians and Suryanis who were not from the same religion, were the representatives of the Monophozit Christians. There had been a contrary and difference of beliefs between the Byzantines and the Monophozit Christians, since the Council of Kadıköy was held in 451. These differences were based on the Armenian understanding of Christianity. Because the Gregorian Christians were the representatives of a branch of Chris-

---

[1] For the tolerance of the Turks towards Greek Orthodox Christians and their Churches see; M. Süreyya Şahin, *Fener Patrikhanesi ve Türkiye*, İstanbul 1980, p. 35-38.

tianity that was presented by Kirkor (Gregoir), who was a Turk, lso this type of Christianity had some national characteristics dominated by Turkish culture. This Christianity was distinguished by its beliefs, style of worshipping, religious ceremonies, church music and applications from other Christian sects. Kirkor brought different ethnic subjects such as Hays, Pers, Greeks, Georgians and the Turks all together under the umbrella of Christianity called as "Gregorian Christianity", in a region called Armenia. He constructed a Church, in which some similarities, even some common things of Turkish culture to the Gregorian Christianity was explained as a sect dominated by Turkish culture.[2]

The Armenians who were the Gregorian Christians, accepted Christians in masses in 301, but didn't participate in religious disputes untill 451. The religious disputes started when Emperor, Constantineple gave freedom of Christianity was tried to be solved by the Councils. However, each Council caused another dispute. During the meetings, which aimed to end the disputes and to determine Christian beliefs, various ideas appeared and the ones which weren't accepted gave rise to other conflicting ideas. In the Council of Kadıköy, in 451, the dogma which supported that Jesus was the unique and only son of God and also that two kinds of charactersistics united in him was accepted

[2] See; Abdurrahman Küçük, *Ermeni Kilisesi ve Türkler*, Ankara 1997, p. 1-10; 297-299.

which conflicted with the decisions taken in the Council of Ephesus, in 431. These characteristics were explained as "united among themselves, undivided and unchanged". Christians claimed that both divine and human characteristics united in Jesus and formed one nature called "Monophisit". This term came into general use among the Christians. Gregorian Christians were among the representatives of this Monophisit dogma. Monophisit Christians were kept under pressure by both administrative and sovereign Christian centres.[3] The Byzantine Empire believed that the representation of Christianity was vested in them and so applied pressure to the groups accepting the Christian beliefs under their domination. They used brutal force aginst the groups which weren't accepting Christian beliefs. Christians who didn't accept the dominant understanding of Christianity were oppressed. Among these groups of people were the Armenians who belonged to a different culture and had a different understanding of Christianity. Also there were the Gregorian Christians.

---

[3] Moise de Khoréne, "Histoire d' Arménie ", (book III, part LXI). Translated to French by Victor Langlois, *Collection des Historien Ancienset Modernes de l'Armenie*, Paris 1880, I /185-186; Malachie Ormanian, *L'Eglise Arménienne*, Paris 1954, 14-17, 24-28; Muhammed Ebu Zehra, *Conferrances on Christianity*, Translator: Akif Nuri, Istanbul 1978, 224-253; Francis Dvornik, *Konsiller Tarihi, İznik'ten II. Vatikana*, Translator: Mehmet Aydın, Ankara 1990, p. 3-18.

The Byzantine Empire identified itself with the Orthodox belief after the Greek culture. The Byzantine Empire used means of force and presure in order to impose their own culture and beliefs on their subjects. The Armenians accepted Monophizit beliefs and claimed that they represented Christianity in its purest form also claimed velemently that their churches were autonomos. Gregorian Armenians didn't accept the demands of the Byzantine Empire because they feared of being lost between Christianity and Orthodoxy. This rejection resulted in the Byzantines acting very brutally and harshly towards the Gregorian Armenians. The result was a continuous dispute and hostility between the Gregorian Armenians and the Orthodoxy Church.[4]

Another reason for this hostility was caused because during the period when the Zoroasters were forced on the Armenians by the Persians who tried to impose their own culture to the Armenians by brutal force which resulted in a war. The Armenians got no support from the Byzantines in this war although they were trying to preserve Christianity. The Armenians demanded help from them but were rejected by Emperor Marcien. The Armenians hated the

[4] *Urfalı Mateos Vekayinamesi*, Translator: H. D. Andreasyan, Ankara 1962, pp. 110-113, 128-129; Jacque de Morgan, *Histoire de L'Arménie*, Paris 1919, p. 162; G. Ostrogorsky, *Bizans Devleti Tarihi*, Translator: Fikret ışıltan, Ankara 1981, pp. 47-48, 50-57; Louis Brehier, *Vie et Mort de Byzance*, Paris 1969, p. 61.

Emperor and his subjects as a result they didn't help them and just watched the happennings because of these problems the Armenians could never trust the Byzantines and the hostility between them continued.

Their conversion to Christianity resulted in the seperation of the Armenians and the Persians but it couldn't bring them under the Latin and Greek sovereignty. Armenian bishops hated the Greek priests because they were following a sly policy. The situation was also the same for the Greek priests. This mutual hostility increased with the decision taken by the Armenian Katogikos, Babgen who gathered the Council of Bishops in 506. From this time onwards, the Armenian Church definitely separated from the Greek Church. The Armenian Church, which had beliefs different from other Christian Churches remained independent, isolated and national. However, Justinian (527-565), who was an influential person in the church, and as being in favour of real belief, wanted to end the religious disputes and especially Monophisitism between the Armenians and the Byzantines. According to him, the task of the government was to preserve Orthodoxy and also further its domination. That's why he tried his best to give some privildges to the Monophizits, but all his effort was fruitless. Armenians, faced with harsher pressure and oppression from the Greek Priests them from Justinien, took the protection of Orthodoxy. From time to time, the Byzantines (the Greeks) tried their best to win the decisions of the Council of Kadıköy in order to take the Gregorian Armenians to their side.

The Byzantines promised that if the Gregorian Christians converted to the belief of Orthodoxy, their political situation would be improved. Also, the Byzantines tried to attain tehir goals by adopting obedient patriarchs. The religious policies of the emperors, their influences and their actions were all in vain because according to the class of Armenian Priests, the existence of an autonomous Armenian Church was a condition to preserve their national unity[5] and they believed that unification with the Byzantines would be the end of them. Emperor Heraklius brought the Armenian bishops and the Greeks together in 629. He wanted them to merge and also aimed to find a way to negotiate in terms of beliefs between the Byzantines and the Gregorian Armenians. These bishops negotiated on some subjects however, the Greek bishops forced Armenian Bishops to accept Byzantine beliefs and disciplines. They also wanted the Armenian bishops to remove "dogmatic disagrements" which were seperating them from the "Universal Church". These two demands were the result of the privileges given by the Armenian bishops. The Ar-

---

[5] Ormanian, *ibid*, p. 25-31; K. Aslan, *L'Arménie et les Arméniens*, İstanbul 1919, p. 38-40, p. 48-50; François Tournebize, *Histoire Politique et Religiuse de L'Arménie*, Paris 1900, p. 93; J. de Morgan, p. 109; Ahmed Refik, *Tarih-i Umum-î*, İstanbul 1327, p. IV /115.

menians rejected such an agreement because they regarded it as atheism.[6]

Emperor Konstant II (641-663), who came to throne after Heraklius, was very angry at the Gregorian Armenians as they followed the same beliefs but didn't accept unification. He tried to annex their territories and force them to accept Orthodox belief, but he wasn't successful in practice of his religious policies.[7]

The Muslims appeared at the time when the Greeks began to keep the Christians under their control, forcing them to accept the beeliefs of Orthodoxy as they regarded themselves as the uniqe authority. Tolerance of the Muslims towards the people from other religions allowed approchement with the Christians, especially the Armenians towards the Muslims as they were exhausted from Byzantine oppression. Muslims gave religious fredom to the Armenians and took them under their control. Konstant II got very angry as the Valis appointed by the Byzantines joined the Muslim Caliphates. Konstant II tried to keep them under control by force and pressure. The Anger of the emperor was calmed by the intervention of the religious leaders. The religious leaders forced the Gregorian Armenians for unifica-

[6] F. Tournebize, *ibid*, p. 95-96.
[7] J. de Morgan, *ibid*, p. 117; Tournebize, p. 97.

tion of their doctrines. The Armenians were under great pressure and oppression. The Muslim soldiers rescued the Gregorian Armenians from this torture and gave them full independence in their religion. They provided them suitable conditions in which they coulde keep their religious differences.[8]

Justinien II (668-669), again wanted to control the Armenians who were under Muslim sovereignty but the Gregorian Armenians responded. The Gregorian Armenians said "Whenever we were subservient to the Greeks, they never helped us. Our loyalty and obedience caused our destruction and declination. Therefore leave us under the sovereignty of the sovereigns (Muslim masters) who protected and supported us".[9]

In the Gregorian Armenians this response caused some disorder as the Byzantine army was pressurizing on them. Thousands of people were harshly tortured, some were sold as slaves and the others who didn't accept Orthodoxy were tortured. This religious intolerance continued which casused continuos hatred among the Gregorian Armenians and the Byzantines which never estinguished.[10] Differences in beliefs and their practices played an important role

[8] Tournebize, *ibid*, p. 97; M. Ormania, *ibid*, p. 45-37; F. Ovornik, p. 22.

[9] Jean VI. Catholicos, from chp. XIII. J. de Morgan, *ibid*, p. 117.

[10] J. de. Morgan, *ibid*, p. 117-118.

in the disaggreement between the Churches and caused them to defend their beliefs and traditions.

The Churches with the support from the Byzantines didin't respect other Churches inferior to them and did not pay attention to their beliefs and practices. After the Monophists, this situation caused the seperation of the Christian world into two communities, east and west in 1054. Eastern church claimed itself as "Orthodoxs" while the Western Church maccepted itself as "Catholic". Rome became the center of the Western Church; Constantinople became the centre of the Eastern Church. The disputed period between East and West began after this certain division. In addition to this, a competition between these Churches started to influence the Autonomus and national Churches. In order to control them they increased their pressure and cruelty over them. Phoius (Fotius), the Patriarch of Constantinople tried to make benefit from autonomy of the Armenian Church and he tried to make them accept the decison taken in the Kadıköy Council, in the religious disputes Roman Church and them. But he wasn't successful. In spite of this, there were some people among the Gregorian Armenians who leaned towards "the Doctrine of Greek-Orthodoxy" but this caused a dispute among the Armenians. Armenian Katogichos was tolerated after the annexation of Ani by Byzantine, but later on he was exiled to Istanbul and died there. During 1054, Katogichos Khakik II from Ani was forced to convert into the belief of Byzantine Orthodoxy. He was called to

Istanbul for this reason and was tortured. Katogichos was exiled to Thavblour three years later (1054-1057) and he died there in 1060.[11]

Appearance of the Turks in Anatolia and their victory over the Byzantines were the beginning of a new era for the Christian minorities, especially for the Gregorian Armenians. The conquest of Anatolia by a Turk Sultan Alpaslan after his uncle, Tuğrul Beg and his turning towards Constantinople calmed down the Armenians. Also this situation provided safety to the Armenians from the Greek torture and they felt relieved. However, then Byzantine struggled aginst the Armenians. Mateos from Urfa claimed his struggle that; "This time they hated, fighting and heroism and investigated Armenian sact. They caused disorder in the church. They hesitated from fighting aginst the Persians but they were trying to influence the real Christians, they wanted them to turn over their own beliefs. Whenever they found a brave and strong man aginst them, they either killed him or tortured him. After the death of Katogichos Bedros, Romans increased their cruelty. Also they started to attack to the Holy office (Eçmiyazin Church). They wanted to bring the Armenians to a false sect called as Kalkedon by removing this holy place..."[12]

[11] M. Ormania, *ibid*, p. 37-48; F. Duornik, *ibid*, p. 23-31; G. Ostrogorsky, *ibid*, p. 153-170.
[12] *Urfalı Mateos Vekâyinamesi*, p. 112-113.

Greeks people and the group of Priests despised the Armenians and behaved them cruelly. Even in Kapadoccia, Greeks despised eastern Christians (the Armenians) who didn't belived in God in the way they believed. The best evidence of this is the attitude of Markos, Metropolit of Kayseri, towards the Armenians. This Bishop was influencial and famous among the Greeks. He showed his hostility towards the Armenians by naming his dog as "Armen" and calling the Armenians as "Dogs". The Armenian king, Gagik heard about this and got extremely angry and when he heard that the emperor wanted to baptisehis nobles as Romans, his sadness increased. Gagik decided not to go to the emperor as he trusted the Turkish Sultan, Alpaslan. Therefore he ordered the Armenian soldiers to attack and rape the Roman women in order to provoke the Greeks. After this happenning, Gogik decided to live under the rule of the Turkish Sultan, Alpaslan. However as he was Christian he was afraid to live under the domination of a Muslim Emperor. But as the time passed, the tolerance shown by the Turks towards the Armenians affected them as the Greeks, although being Christians tortuered them. So they were happy under the rule of the Muslim Turks.

Gagik went to the house of Metropolit Markos, which was in Kayseri, in order to take revenge from him and he stayed there as a guest. Metropolit Markos took him to his house with a great ceremony and gave a banquet in his honor. By this time Gogik said "We wish to see the dog". Gogik ignored, even on tehir great insistance it didn't come. But later on when they called its name "Armen, it came". Gogik asked Markos "has this dog got the name Armen?". Markos shield and answered hesitantly "we call it as Armen as it is a puppy". Then Gogik said "we will see either the Armenians or the Greeks are childs". He order that Matropolit and his dog should be put in the same sack. The dog was killed by hitting and Markos was killed as well. After that he ordered markos's property to be looted.[13]

Another event took place before this event in 1066, which showed the hostility of another Emperor Ducas (Dugite) and his subjects towards the Armenians. Emperor Ducas, Patriarch Jean Xiphilin, the Statesmen and all of the Priests thought, unanimously, to remove Armenian sect and to supress the belief of Saint Gregoire Lusavorich. Also they aimed to remove Armenian Church with its practices and wanted to impose their own practices of beliefs on them. Firstly, Emperor Ducas sent a massage to Sivas to call Atom and Apusah, who were the Armenian royalists to Constantinople. They took Hugopos Varbet, who was an expert on holy books, along with them. The emperor said "You and all Armenian leaders should be baptised according to the Roman sects". The Armenian royalists answered that "We can not decide about anything without asking to Gogik, the son of Asot. As he is a wise man, our king and our groom, so we should ask him first. So call him here or else he will put us

[13] *Urfalı Mateos Vekâyinamesi*, p. 131-132.

in fire if we do something without him". The Emperor didn't want Gogik to come. But Atom and Apusah informed Gagik by sending a man to them. Then Gagik came to Constantinople and they explained Armenian belief in the presence of the emperor.[14]

Gogik protected the superiority of the Armenian Church's beliefs and doctrines, its truth and "Apostic" character, as Byzantines (Greeks and Latin) accepted their beliefs as superior and despised Armenians beliefs.[15]

Kevork Aslan, an Armenian author, claimed that the Greek Priests always degraded the Armenians. Due to their cruelity Armenian Priests and the public became hostile towards the Byzantines. For this reson, instead of defending their empire they were quite moderate towards the Turks, Persians and the Muslim Arabs.[16]

Byzantine annexed the kingdom of Ani in 1054. They tortured the Armenians in a very cruel manner, they imposed high taxes, attacked their religions asso-

---

[14] *Urfalı Mateos Vekâyinamesi*, p. 128-129. For Gagiks defence of the Doctrine of The Armenian Church see; *Chronique de Mathieu d'Edesse*, Par Ed. Dulauriet, Paris 1858, p. 133. (This defense of Gagik didn't take place in Turkish translation of and reasyan. and reasyan didn't translated this part as it is religious and just skipped it over by "... ").

[15] *Chronique de Matthieu, ibid*, p. 134-151.

[16] K. Aslan, *ibid*, p. 56.

ciation and exiled the pious people. This hostility and negative attitude continued till the territory was annexed by the Seljuk Turks. The Armenians and the Syrians, who were subjected to Byzantine tyranny, belived that the Turks were sent to them as a gift of the God as to punish the Greeks. For this reason they helped the Turks[17]. After the victory in Malazgirt, Armenians' close relations with the Turks began and they came under the sovereignity of the Turks.*

[17] *Urfalı Mateos Vekâyinamesi*, 11-113; J. de Morgan, *ibid*, p. 154; Osman Turan, *Türk Cihan Hakimiyet Mefkuresi Tarihi*, İstanbul, 1979, II/479; G. Ostrogorsky, *ibid*, p. 309-324; İhsan Sakarya, *Belgelerle Ermeni Sorunu*, Ankara 1984-8.

* Beginning of the Crusades had positive effects on the Greek -Roman Church and the Armenian relations. However, the unification provided in 1198 lasted short. Approchement between the Orthodoxs and the Catholics began with the Crusades. But actually, it hadn't had a long life. During the fourth Crusades, the soldiers who came for the purpose of "Holy Lands "came to Constantinople. They ceased from the Crusade and looted Istanbul. They killed the people who weren't Catholic and tortured them in every respect. The Orthodoxs were subjected to every kind of cruelty. Therefore, the approchement became a reason of greater hostility. For this reason when Istanbul was conquered by the Turks the Orthodoxs said "We prefer to see turban of Turks rather than seeing the cap of the Catholics ". The Orthodox Christians showed their hostility and lack of confidence towards the Byzantines and also showed their friendship and confidence towards the Turks. Armenians took their lesson from this event and preferred the sovereignity of the Turks as they were harmed by the approchement of the Turks with the Christians. This sovereignity continued in the Ottoman period more tolerantly; the saying "If the Armenians had a chance to reach today its by the help of the Turks". This saying clearly proved and symboled out the tolerence of the Turks.

Sultan Alpaslan met with Armenian Giory (Kiuri), who ruled the territory on the behalf of the Byzantine empire. When he reached to the Armenian territory he annexed it with the Byzantine state. Alpaslan made a treaty with Giorg and decided him to pay annual takes and also to give his daugher to him. After the besiege of Ani, by Alparslan, in 1064, Gagik invited the Sultan to Kars to accept his dependence to the Sultan. Gagik, the king of Kars, expressed his acceptence of the Sultan's sovereignity. Therefore, Soulan Alparslan rewarded him with a robe of honour.

Alparslan divided the conquered territory among the emirs who were with him. and he informed other Muslim emirs about the conquests by sending them a fetihname. This news caused cheerfulness in Bagdad and the other Islamic countries. The caliphate gave the name "Ebu'l-Fetih" (father of the conquest) to Sultan Alparslan[18].

Turks continued their marching into Small Asia after the conquest of Ani and they annexed kayseri in 1067.[19] The Greeks (the Roums) who took the Armenians under the sovereignity, defenced the territory by an army consisting of Rums and Armenians aginst the Selchubids. However, these territories were

[18] Kévork Aslan, É'tude Historique sur le Peuple Arménien, Paris 1900, p. 335; Ali Sevim, Genel Çizgileriyle Selçuklu-Ermeni ilişkileri, Ankara, 1983, p. 15-17.
[19] K. Aslan, ibid, p. 71.

conquered by the Selchukids. In spite of the Rums' counter offensive a few times, the Armenians came under the dominance of the Selchukids and Turk vanguards advanced till the gates of Constantinople.[20]

Momak, who came to the throne during the time when the Byzantines met with the Turks in Anatolia, began to afford Byzantine expenses from the Armenians. Therefore, high taxes were imposed on to them. In addition to this, Armenian notables were driven into the inner parts of Anatolia and he disarmed the Armenians.[21] Except from these, Byzantine notables and Patriarches annexed the Armenian Church and monastries and settled down there. Also religious massacres were results of their effort to remove Gregorian Armenian Church.[22]

Since the centuries because of having different languages, customs, traditions and especially different religious beliefs the hostility of the Byzantines towards the Armenians increased. These differences caused great hostility between the two communities and continued.[23] Armenian and the Syrioc annalists wrote that the Greeks pushed out the Armenaians out of their country and treated them in a vary brutal way.[24] During the time

[20] J. A. Gatteyrias, *L'Arménie et les Arméniens*, Paris 1882, p. 97; K. Aslan, *ibid*, p. 71; Ali Sevim, *ibid*, p. 13-17.

[21] René Grousset, *Histoire de L'Arménie*, Paris, 1947, p. 586-587.

[22] A. Sevim, *ibid*, p. 13.

[23] J. De Morgan, *ibid*, p. 162.

42

that Byzantines had dominated the Armenians and tortured them, the public never dealth with the Byzantine Empire. Also at this time, the Turks began to threat the Byzantine Empire. The Armenians in return of getting rid of the Byzantines wanted to be dominated by the Turks and to live under their domination.[25]

Byzantine emperor, Romen Diyojen attempted to end Alpaslan's advance in Anatolia but he was completely defeated in the Battle of Malazgirt (1071). In this battle, the Byzantines applied pressure on the Armenians to make them accept their beliefs and norms and the Turks were acting them in a very kind way, they were totally free in their beliefs and their religious pratices. Therefore, the Armenians decided under the sovereignity of the turks would be much more better and safer. This was the basic reason why the Armenians didn't supported the Byzantines in the Battle of Malazgirt. They wanted the Turks to defeat the Byzantines and even didn't help the Byzantines during the war.[26]

The Armenians benefited from the decline of the Byzantine Empire. Even time to time they caused

[24] *Urfalı Mateos Vekayînâmesi*, p. 98; Süryanî Mihael, "Chronique", from III /169 Osman Turan, *Selçuklular Tarihi*, p. 183-184.

[25] J. De Morgan, *ibid*, p. 154.

[26] *Urfalı Mateos Vekâyînâmesi*, p. 133-135; O. Turan, *Selçuklular Tarihi ve Türk İslam Medeniyeti*, İstanbul 1980, p. 183-184; K. Aslan, *ibid*, p. 336.

rivals in Anatolia aginst the Byzantines, as they had strained relations with them. These rivals helped the decline of the Byzantine Empire. They regarded the Turks as the savers of their survival. Even some Armenians converted to Islam. The Armenian Bogusas family took permission from Alparslan[27] to settle down in a place near to Siverek. Alparslan was succeeded by his sonMelikşah. The Selchukids gained the territory from India till the Caspian Sea and the Straits.[28] Also the Armenians felt totally relieved by coming under the sovereignity of the Selchukids.[29]

After the death of Alparslan, there occured some rebellions in some places but the rebellious people were subdued by increasing the taxs prices. Although they forgot about how tolerant the Turks were and caused rebellions, Turks still did not tortured them and did not put limitations to their beliefs, religious practices and properties. The Armenian Ani Katoğikos wanted the Selchukids to reduce the taxes. Sultan Melikşah missed his delegates well and gave a decree to Barseğ. This decree stated that "the office of the Armenian Katogichos would be represented by a unique office and all Churches, Monastries and spiritual people were exampted from taxation..." Then taxation was removed, Armenian towns were reconstructed and the Armenian Churches and

[27] A. Sevim, *ibid*, p. 18.
[28] J. De Morgan, *ibid*, p. 154; K. Aslan, *ibid*, p, 171.
[29] F. Tournebize, *ibid*, p. 136-137.

Monastries were taken under the protection of the Selchukids.[30] The Armenian author, Urfalı Mateos, presented the tolerance of Sultan Melikşah in his sentences that the Sultans death was described. "At the same year, Sultan Melikşah, father of all, merciful to all who had good opinions about all, died... Death of Melikşah caused a great grief in the whole world..."[31]

Religious and administration tolerance continued in the period of Turkeish Selchukids as it was during the period of great Selchukids. In spite of this, Armenians rebelled aginst the Turks by the beginning of the Crusades. The rebellions happened sometimes by the encouragement of the Crusades and sometimes by that of the Byzantines. Although they had re-accepted seljuk domination, after the establishment of Seljuk sovereignity they started rebelling time to time. However they always repented for the rebellions they caused. They promised to remain loyal to the Turks as they were always tolerent and kind to them. Later on a harmonial arena was established between the Turks and the Christians in Anatolia.[32]

[30] *Urfalı Mateos Vekâyînâmesi*, p. 176 –177; F. Tournebize, *ibid*, p. 137-138; A. Sevim, *ibid*, p. 20.

[31] *Urfalı Mateosu'un Vekayinamesi*, p. 178.

[32] O. Turan, *Selçuklular Tarihi*, p. 238, 353-354; O. Turan, *Türk Cihan Hâkimiyeti, II.*, p. 477-480; J. A. Gatteyrias, *ibid*, p. 98-108; A. Sevim, *ibid*, p. 26-29, 39-40; Faruk Sümer, "Çukurova Tarihi", *Tarih Araştırmaları Dergisi*, Ankara 1963, volume I., nr. 1, p. 5-19.

The Turks tolerated all of the non-muslims; They were appreciate by not only the people inside their borders but also the people abroad; they helped the Armenians to get rid of the Byzantine's financial and religious tyrannythey had their old, Turkish nomadic l and administration tradition; they obeyed to Islam's conquest laws. According to Osman Turan, all the above stated facts are related with the non-muslim's appreciation of the Turks.[33]

These caused the most of the Armenians to prefer the Turkish judges rather then the Christian judges and axxepted Turkish sovereignity by their own dem and s. Religious and political tolerance of Ottoman Principality towards the Armenians continued as it did to all Muslims. The Armenians, who were living in the Caucas, Eastern Anatolia and Clicia as dispersed at the beginning of the fourteenth century, were under the administration of the Persians, Byzantines and the Selchukids. During that time, there were a few Armenians settled aroud Söğüt, near to the Ottoman Principality. After the annexation of Bursa, Osman Gazi made it Bursa the capital and brought the Armenians and the religious leaders from Kütahya and to Bursa.

The Armenians were attracted by the Seljuk Turks because of the religious and political pressures of the Byzantines. As they relied on the Ottomans,

---

[33] O. Turan, *Türk Cihan Hâkimiyeti II*, p. 478-480.

they spreaded out towards West and they began to serve for the Ottomans as a result of the Greeks and Latins religious and political oppressions. The Armenians, who won the trust of the Turks, were rewarded by privileges which thry had never seen before. This privileges were given from the time of Osman Beg and also continued during the time of Fatih Sultan Mehmet. Even when he conquered Istanbul, in order to have reliable subjects there, brought many Armenians from different parts of Anatolia and settled them. Sultan Mehmet,the conquerer didn't interfered to Armenians religious and internal affairs and additionally gave many privileges to them along with the Greeks. He invited Metropolit of Bursa, Bishop Hovakim to Istanbul; he established the Armenian Patriachate and made him the Bishop Patriarch. He increased his influence by binding the Suryanis, Copts, Georgians, Abyssin, ans and the people from Kalde to the Armenian Patriarchate.[34]

The Chief Priest Karakin Kazancian, the the leader writer of the Review "Sogagat" stated in his

[34] Archives of Prime-ministry, Yıldız Classification, part 34, document nr: 299. envelope 27 k. 79; M. Ormanian, *ibid*, p. 60-61; Esat Uras, *Tarihte Ermeniler ve Ermeni Meselesi*, İstanbul 1987, p. 149; Fuat Köprülü, *Edebiyat Araştırmaları*, Ankara 1966, p. 250-253; O. Turan, *Selçuklular Tarihi*, p. 152, 162; Avram Galanti, *Türkler ve Yahudiler*, İstanbul 1977, p. 16; Abdurrahman Küçük, "Ermeni Katoğikosluğu ve Ermeni Meselesine Dair Bir Arşiv Vesikası Üzerine", *A.Ü. İlahiyat Fakültesi Dergisi*, XXVI, p. 740.

essay written for the 500 th anniversery of the Conquest of Istanbul, that the Real history of Armenians began with the conquest of Istanbul. Also according to his determination, Sultan the conquerer visited Armenian Bishop Hovoakim in his house while he was in Bursa. He said to the Bishop that he thought hard about the conquest of Istanbul. After listening carefully, the Bishop said "I wish God will make your kingdom sacred and makes it spread to the whole world "and then he got the sword of the Sultan and prayed for a whole weak.[35] These sources are gathered from the researches of the Armenian authors. Another Armenian author, Papazin stated that as the Armenians believed that Jesus had "a nature", they couldn't practice their "Messe" (Bread-Wine) Ceremony and the way of their worships freely, during the Byzantine period. For this reason, they wanted the conquest of Istanbul by the Turks.[36]

Yavuz Sultan Selim conquered Jerusalem while he was marching towards Eygpt after he defeated the Memlüks, in 24th of August 1516. There were Muslims with Christians including Gregorians Armenians among the people who welcomed him in Jerusalem. During this time Yavuz Sultan Selim had given

---

[35] Karekin Kazancian, "Les Arméniens Aprés la Conquète", *La Turquie Modern*, Juin Juillet 1953, s. 91.

[36] Hrant Papazian, *L'Eglises Byzantines Transferées aux Arméniens*, İstanbul 1976, p. 7-8.

privileges to the Armenians.[37] After the Çaldıran victory, the Sultan also brought many Armenians artisans to Istanbul from Tabriz.[38]

The Armenians lived a comfortable and peaceful life under the sovereignity of the Turks, during the period from the Selchukids till the reign of Mahmut II. Their social and religious affairs were never interfered; they practiced their religious beliefs and ceremonies freely, in their own temples. They were occupied with trade and industry and became very rich. Their population also increased as they were exempted from military service. They totally focused on education, as they were more advantaged compared to the Turkish subjects. Therefore, many Armenians served at high ranks in the Ottoman state. When the period of decline began in the Ottoman Empire, some of the subjects who seemed obedient took up a contrary position towards the Ottomans. The Armenian Church which was supported, protected from annihilation and from being lost among other Churches started to take active parts in political activities and naturally began to religious and

[37] Selahattin Tansel, *Yavuz Sultan Selim*, Ankara 1969, p. 160-196.

[38] E. Uras, *ibid*, p. 149.

The best example of the tolerance of the Turks towards the Armenians is that there were Armenians in the Ottoman Administration, during the so called "The Armenian issue", (see; Archives of Prime-ministry, Yıldız, k. 36, document 368, 20, 141, ka. XII).

political actions aginst the Turks. Eventually, an "Armenian Problem" appeared.[39]

Malchia Ormania, who served as the Armenian Patriarck in Istanbul, has a book called as *L'Eglise Armenienne*. In his book, he explained the tolerance shown to the Armenians by the Turks and the privileged position of the Armenians in the Ottoman Empire. In the forward of this book's first edition, we can shortly summerize Bertrand Bareilles (1910) as that, the Turks didn't make any changes in the positions of the people under their domination. They were contented with impossing the orders of the Holy Book, Qur'an. Quran ordered the Muslims to prepare a circumstance to the people who were living under their domination, in which they can own their property by paying tributes. Christians who benefited from this atmosphere, were organizing well and they were living their own life freely by obeying Turkish administration.

The Patriarches who were given delegation from by the Ottoman Empire became the chief of the Armenians. This chief was responsible to the government. He was collecting taxes through his officers

[39] E. Uras, *ibid*, p. 149-150; *A Qui La Faute? Aux Partis Revolutionnaires Armeniens*, İstanbul 1917, p. 40-52; Pierre A. Moser, *Arméeins oûest La Realite?*, Libraire Lallier 1980, p. 19-20; K. Gürün, *ibid*, p. 54-62.

who were under his controll and guarantee. Nearly all kinds of trials from civil and criminal issues till the religious ones were dealth within the court of the Patriarchate. Sultan Mehmet the Conquerer, had given such privileges to the Patriarch Gennadius, which was never given to any minority untill that time. The Armenians were among the first who supported the Sultan in his reform movements.[40]

In spite of all kind intention of the Turks aginst the Armenians, most of the Armenians didn't stay loyal to the Turks. Their loyalty and obedience were only seen durimg the period when the Ottomans were powerfull. Howevere during the state of decline the Armenians showed their real face. Until the 18 th century there weren't any events occuring about the Armenias. Armenians had their own education system and attempts which caused the appetite of some Armenians and also the Christian missionaries. As a result of this, Catholic missionaries began their activities among Gregorian Armenians. These caused some people to tend to Catholicism and caused their Christian sects to be changed. These activities made the Armenian Church ancious, so the Church dem and ed Ottoman government to take measures. The necessary measures which were taken didn't work. The missionary activities spreaded nearly to every field like education and press. The missionary Bishops who were trown out from Istanbul spreaded over some centres in the East, South-east and central Anatolia and began to open some schools in those areas. Later on some Bishops from Amrica and England and joined the Catholic Bishops.[41]

After the Catholics, at the beginning of the 19th century (1928), the British started animating Armenian Churches in Istanbul, İzmir, Ankara, Kayseri, Antakya, Gaziantep, Arapkir, Harput and also Erzurum and also started opening schools. According to the decision taken by the American Board Organization,[42] in 1832, they tried to improve the Armenian Churches in Kayseri, Gaziantep, Diyarbakır, Bursa, Maraş, Sivas, Tokat, Trabzon, Erzurum and Harput.[43] The Armenians were seen as an open gate to enter Turkey. Some Countries like Amrica and Russia forced this gate and aimed to enter Turkey. The idea of being minority was imposed on the Armenians, who were the most loyal subject to the Ottomans. The

[41]Abdurrahman Küçük, "Belgelerin Işığında Türk-Ermeni Münasebetlerine Genel Bakış" *A.Ü İlahiyat Fakültesi Dergisi*, Ankara. 1989, XXX, p. 248.

[42] For American Missionaries, American Board Organization and its activities see; Uygur Kocabaşoglu, *Kendi Belgeleriyle Anadolu'daki Amerika*, İstanbul, 1989; İlknur Polat Haydaoğlu, *Osmanlı İmparatorluğunda Yabancı Okullar*, Ankara 1990, p.127-150, 196-210.

[43] E. Kırşehirlioğlu, *Türkiye'de Misyoner Faaliyetleri*, p. 33; İ. Sakarya, *ibid*, p.25.

American Board Organization affected the Armenians trough the schools and by the books which were distributed, they tried to provocate them.[44]

During the Armenian rebellion aginst the Turks, in November 1890, an "ariza" (a kind of document) was offered to the Sultan. This ariza included signature of thirty-six influenced traders and bankers. Also Agop Pasha, the Minister of Finance, Orhan Efendi the Councillor of Justice, Concillor of Forign affairs and assistant and members of various courts signed this document. They reproached the movements aginst the Turks in this ariza and they the situation as that "some people ventured into illegal publishing and business all around, for the purpose of disintegrating the Armenian subjects which were under the domination of the Ottomans and who were devoted since ancient times. Therefore, they worked naively by serving to a harmful idea to the safety and benefits of Loyal Armenian Community. "As people who did such actions were minorities, they couldn't represent the Armenians. Loyal Armenian Community hadn't already showed consideration and repect to their ideas". The Armenians had acuired happiness and comfort by protecting their religion and language under the domination of the Turks, since 500 years. From

[44] E. Kırşehirlioglu, *ibid*, p. 29; Necdet Sevinç, *Ajan Okulları*, İstanbul 1975, p. 40-50; K. Gürün, *Ermeni Dosyası*, Ankara 1983, p. 41.

this time on, they hadn't any doubt about compassion and justice of the state and they would continue their loyalty and service to the Empire. These were also stated in the ariza.[45] We can see how much the Turks relied on the Armenians, how much the Armenians were given privileges and also how much the Turks tolerated the Armenians, when we saw the signatures and their owners' ranks in these documents, called ariza.

The other documents that presented the tolerance of the Turks, are the essays written during the Armenian revolts aginst the Turks. These essays were printed in the view of "Dadjar". The summery of this review essays was printed by the Armenians in French, by the name "A qui La Faute? Aux Partis Revolutionnaire Armenians" (whose is the fault? In the Armenian Revolotionary Parties), in 1917[46]. Information in this book is a kind of "confession document", presenting tolerance of Turkish nation, despite of all negotiations. I want to conclude the subject, "tolerance of the turks towards the Armenians", by some paragraphs taken from that book:

"Although real task of these Armenian Revolutionary Parties was to move for benefit of Turkey

[45] Başbakanlık Arşivi; Yıldız k. 36, ev, 368, 20. 141. ka. XIII.
[46] *A Qui La Faute? Aux Partis Revolutionnaire Armenies*, İstanbul, 1917.

and to serve her, they collaborated with Russian administration which was an enemy and a insidious government."[47]

"Armenian Revolutionary Parties established secret relations with enemies of Turkey after the war began. They betrayed the most sacred benefits of Turkey, as they met with Russian ambassador about reformation of six provinces."[48]

"Russians goverment, exectioner of the revolutionary parties befor, became their protector today…American-Turk fraternity was so hearty and close that Russia, our protector today, was torturing Cousasus Americans at that time… There are two reasons why Russia behave so: 1- Turk and American friendship wasn't suitable for Russian policy and intention. Russian diplomacy which couldn't find any excuse to interfere with internal affairs of Turkey went to bankrupt in the markets of Ottoman government. 2- The Americans who were in the East and West sides of Russia could come together with the people who were in eastern provinces of Turkey and from the same generation and they could disturb Russian Tzars. Americans inside Russia could agitate Russia by taking side against him. This was a worrying and threatening situation. Russia couldn't

---

[47] *ibid*, p. 9.
[48] *ibid*, p. 16.

accept Turk-American harmany. Because in all Ottoman cabinets followed each other, after the Constitution, there was an American Minister."[49]

"Religious communities had become revolution guilds of Armenian revolutionary parties, for a long time and their the most devilish plans were prepared there. Religious centers became weapon stores and conspiracy guilds... Religious ledaers were ancouraging people who relied on them to rebel, by their speaking and writing. Holy words and the doctrine of the New Testament weren't mentioned in preaches, any longer;rebellian instead of loyalty and honesty, grudge and revenge instead of humanity, humility and disseputableness instead of morality were being preached... Religious leaders were heading ceremonies, meetings, festivals organized by committees and wanted people to obey travining and orders of the parties"[50]

"The highest religious leader of all the Armenians Kotochicos Eçmiyazın and charged a private delegation to solve the reform issue. The patriarchate, took a special attitude which wasn't from it's traditions. Armenian Patriarch was always in the sublime Porte to make some objecdtions about reform projects, in each visit of Russian representative there"[51]

---

[49] *ibid*, p. 63.
[50] *ibid*, p. 40-41.
[51] *ibid*, p. 51-52.

"Neither the highest religious leader of the Armenians, nor Katochicos of Eçmiyazin, nor high churh outhoritatives who claimed that they shouldered the destiny of the Armenians nor outhoritative chiefsof this revolutionaryparty, nor other Armenians neither explained nor underst and that we weren't able to protect our existence under any other domination except from Turkey"[52]

"Are there any eample of such a terrible betraying to the Ottoman Empire, a state had which protected the whole society for six centuries and respected their language and national traditions?How can we qualify such hostile and anarchic events, how can we find a rightful reason for such conspiracy tending to murder."[53]

"The Armenian had lived next to the Turk in Turkey for six centuries with a wide religious and social freedon that any other subjects of a nation never saw under any other nation's domination in the world."[54]

b) Religious Tolerance of the Turks Towards the Jews

There had been a dispute, a hostility between Jews and christians since the crucifiction of the Jesus.

---

[52] *ibid*, p. 41.
[53] *ibid*, p. 41.
[54] *ibid*, p. 70.

According to christians unigue responsible for the crucifiction was Jews. This understanding sometimes reached cursing and this took place among the subjects of christian religious ceremonies. This understanding continued till the second Vatican Council (1962-1965) and a decision to starting to have diologue with the Jews was taken in this council. There were some practices, based on force, violence even hostility, among Christian's attitude towards Jews, an hostility was seen after christianity became official state religion.

Attitude of the state, the church and public towards the Jews had changed on a large scale since the Byzantine Emperor Constantine gave freedom to christianity in 313. Byzantine emperors after Constantin make laws against the jews. Life of Jews was limited, they were deteriorated and pounded by these laws. Even Constantine be murdered and converting to Jewish belief was a crime. Constantius, son of Constantin followed his father's way and put capital punishment for inter-marriages between Jews and Christians. During the time of Teodosius (408-450) important changes against Jews were made. He collected all laws made since the time of Constantin I (in 438) and organized them. Statue of Jews was determined clearly by these laws and it's proved that "Jews was a crazy, disgust, sinner nation which should be hated. "Sinagogs" were expelled outside the city, their with essing againts christians was prevented, reading "Mişne" was banned and the Bible could be read just in Greek and Latin.[55]

Jews from time to time faced to face with a difficulty to prefer death or baptise in places under christian sovereignity. They preferred mostly being baptise.[56] Therefore there existed a community consisting of Jews who changed their religion in Spain. They were called as "Konverso" or "Marrano". Jews, in Spain, converted to christianity but they made their Jewish belief continue secretly, asd it happaned in different times and countries. Chararecteristic separates these people changed their religion from other christians that they live like a christians outside but they live like Jews secretly inside their houses. They as a group of people who changed their religion could take place in high position of administration, by another idently. This and their secret continvation of being Jews closely occupied the state. The state and the church came together to solve this issue, in 1464. They established a commission of there to underst and whether "new christians" became really christians or not and to determine which of them made their Jewish beliefs continue. People among "new christians" who was still secretly still Jewish were seized and executed.[57]

[55] Moshe Sevilla-Sharon, *Türkiye Yahudileri*, Jarusalem 1982, p. 5-6.

[56] Moshe Sevilla-Sharon, *ibid*, p. 11.

[57] Moshe Sevilla-Sharon, *ibid*, p. 17-18.

The QDosyaqueen of Casttilia, İsabella and the king of Aragon catholic Ferdinand married in 1469 and their states united. This event was a beginning of an end for the Jews in Spain. Because İsabella and Ferdinand want the Jews to leave the country in three months, by a decree due to they would solve the problem of Jews changing religion. These developments forced the Jews to migrate from Spain. None of the Christian states helped the Jews. The Turk's came to the assistance of the Jews repelled from Spain. There had been Jewish people under the dominance of the Turks, since the period of Selchukids and they had been living a comfortable life. The Jews had known about the Turks and their tolerance However, Jewish migration to Turkish countries accured from Spain.[58]

Settlement of Jews in groups on Turkısh lands was after 1492. However, there was a small group of Jews before that year. Close relations between the Turks and the Jews began by the conguests of Syria and Palestine by the Turks. These relations increased by the establishment of inquisitorial courts in 1203 and by christian appresion to the Jews. After that year, the Jews were tortured in all parts of the world and they were exiled. The Turks came into assistance of the Jews in that period of torture and excile.[59]

[58] Moshe Sevilla-Sharon, *ibid*, p. 15-17; p. 116-117; p. 120-121.
[59] Hikmet Tanyu, *Tarih Boyunca Yahudiler ve Türkler*, İstanbul, 1976. I/110-111, p. 140.

The Jews had lived under presure, torture and cruelty left Bursa as they thought that one more example of bad treatment would be added to previous ones. However, later they saw how good and tolerant people the Turks were and they came back to Bursa. After a short time, the Jews around came to Bursa. When Süleyman Pasha, son of Orhan Bey took Gallipoli and when Murat Bey took Ankara, they met with a small Jewish community. But Murat Beg meet with a big one in Edirne. Edirne became religious and trade center of the Jews in Thrace, while Salonica became that of the Jews in Makedonia. These two centers became so famous that they became subjects for poems, as the time passed. Also Salonica was recognized as mother of Israel. All these were evaluted as a display that the Turks didn't interfere with social and religious issues of people under their dominance. Because, the Turks gave a complete freedom of religion and thought; they didn't interfere with their workships, ceremonies. This attitude made the Jews relaxed and brought them presence. Before they thought that" Islamic zealous" would cause their disappearance. The Jews realized the value of secured atmosphere well, they turned towards trade and became rich, while the Turks were always fighting. The Turks greeted their richness with tolerance.[60]

[60] Avam Galanti, *Türkler ve Yahudiler*, İstanbul 1947, p. 8-10; Leon Sciacky, *Travel to Salanico*, New York 1946, p. 108-116; Abdurrahman Küçük, *Dönmeler Tarihi*, Ankara 1992, p. 70-71.

Close relation and sincerity of Turkish community by a Jewish outhor and Avam Galanti, a Jewish, wrote: Avam Galanti, Türkler ve; Leon Sciacky, Travel to Salonico, Coming of the Turks was the change of situation for them (the Jews) not the change of a dynasty. They considered the Turks as a brother who were close to their religion; not a victorious power and master of ground.[61]

During the Conguest of Istanbul by Mehmet II, the Jews were neutral. This is connected to the fact that they realized before that Byzanline couldn't defense for a long time, in case of an affensive. Also it was because of that the Jews living in the places came under Turkish dominance before such as Dimetoka, Gümülcine, Ohri, Karkarye, Yanbolu informed the others living in Constantinople about Turkish justly administration and religious respect. In this communication translator of the Imperial Chancery of the state of Murat II played a role. Levi spent his youth fulness in Italy, Florence and Pol and. Later he came to Edirne and came under the service of Murad II. He explained to the Jews coming to the Ottoman Palace that the Turks would be dominant power in the future and they were tderant. This made the Ottoman Empire attractive for the Jews in the world.[62]

[61] A. Galanti, *ibid*, p. 10.

[62] Ziya Şakir, "Neşredilmeyen Tarihî Vesikalara göre Türkiye Yahudileri, Fatih Yahudilere İmtiyaz verdi.", *Millet Mecmuası*, 16th October 1947, p. 89.

The tolarance of the Turks towards religious minorities after the conquest of Istanbul, was reached to people who were being fortured especially to the Jews, in every ways. Catholic Administration in Spain said that" The Jews, either be catholic or leave the country". But it was at the same time with time that the Turks introduced their rise and tolerance. In this period there were many Jews living under Turkish diminition. This caused a comporison between the christians and Muslim Turks.

The Jews under Turkish dominance had been living comfortable, while they pressure and cruelty of christian world towards them continued. This situation affect not only the Jews under Turkish dominance but also those living in Spain and Europe. Even many German Jews came to the Ottoman lands by the letter written by Yitzhak Tsarfati, "rabbi"of Eşkinazi, from Edirne.

Rabbi Yitzhak Tsarfati was the leader of Eşkenazi communities livivg in both the Ottoman lands and different parts of central Europe: When two to words the year 1430 religious man visited Rabbi Tsarfati, they saw learly how much good conditions were dominant in the Ottoman lands. and they thought that they could be a solition for the Jews who were being fortured over the world. For this, these religious men wanted Rabbi Tsarfati to write a letter inviting them to the Ottoman Lands to his communites.

He summoned the Jews in Central Europe to come to Turkey, in 1430's.[63]

The letter below is a document which proves the tolerance of the Turks and shows the life style of the Jews living in the Ottoman lands in the 15th century;

"...Our brothers in the country of Aşkenaz, I've heard that Israili people have been suffering from painsworse than death; they are repelled from one city to another; they are subjected to cruelty... Me, loyal, and our modest brother Yitzhak Tsarfati, was born in Aşkenaz (and studied there), while my family was French. However, we had to migrate from my home country and I came here, contry of Togarma. Everything was perfect there. God'd thought this country, very well. Togarma, is on the way going to the country of life (Israel); whole route till Jarusalem is overl and route except from a pass for six miles over sea. Everyday large caravans including Ismaili people (Muslims) and the Jews set on a journey...the route is safe...[64]

Yitzhak Tsarfati saw the country on the way towards Israel that he introduced, as comfortable and everything was perfect there. In the period that he invited his Ottoman country, there was a different approchement in christian world. The Jews were blamed of sacrificing people, dirtying christian's holy

---

[63] Moshe sevilla-Sharon, *ibid*, p. 26-28.
[64] Rozanes, Togorma, from I/20 Sevilla Sharon, *ibid*, p. 26-28.

bread were pursued and they were wanted to be punished as they changed their religion. This was at the some period with the decline of Islamic Girnata State. Also this bears on the fact that acceptance of catholisicm by the Jews in spain was false. King Ferdin and and King Isabella ordered that the Jews would be either catholic or would leave the country. Some of them who didn't inclined to change their left the country. Most of them took refuge with Turkey.[65] Sultan Bayezid II said that "Gates of my country open to all people who are being fortured in any place of the world" and let the Jews enter the Ottoman Empire. His such acceptance was appreciated: "Sultan Bayezid followed his ancestors. If he didn't do so, remainings of the Jews who were repelled from Spain, Aragon, Portugal and sicily and memory of Hz:İbrahim and Israel would be lost..."[66]

Some resources include the evoluation of Sultan Bayezid II about King of Spain, Ferdin and: "Who can say that such a king (Ferdin and, king of Spain) is intelligent? While he is reducing his country to poverty, he is making my country rich".[67] It is expressed that Bayezid II sent messages ordering welcoming of the Jews to all cities and he ordered also about capital punishment of the ones who damaged the Jews.[68] Rabbi

[65] A. Küçük, İbid, p. 97-99.

[66] A. Galanti, Türkler ve Yahudiler, p. 35.

[67] M. Sevilla-Sharon, ibid, p. 30.

Eliya Kapsali explained this issue: "Sultan of Turkey, Bayezid, learnt that Jews in Spain were looking for a shelter as they were harmed. He was merciful, he sent heralds to whole country and banned the forture of the Jews repel of them, definitely. He ordered soft treatment to the Jews and kindly behaviours toward them. Anybody who treated badly to the immigrants or tortured them would be punished by murder".[69]

The reliability of all information is disputed but it was suitable with the occurance of events. Because expressions approve the fact that the Turks were always in favor of inoffersive people. The Turks were always for the weaks and against unjust people. The Jews situation is just an example of this attitucle. The Jews who were tortured in European countries had been migrating in groups to the Ottoman State since the period of Bayezid II. These immigrant Jews were settled in especially important cities of the Ottoman State such as Salonica, Istanbul. Edirne, Bursa. Immigrant Jews who came to these lands before protected late comes and helped them. Not only their religious brother but also state administrators helped and found support. The state banned any kind of bad treatment towards them, in anyway. This is always remembered and documented by the Jews.

[68] M. Sevilla-Sharon, *ibid*, p. 30.

[69] Gilles Viensteini, *L'Empire Ottoman depuis 1492 Jusqu'a la Fin du XIX. é Siecle, les Juifs d'Espagne Dirigé par Henry Mechoulan*, Paris 1992 p. 363.

Turks' tolerance towards the Jews started with the conquest of Bursa and became freguent by the torture in Spain and it lasted till the end of the Ottoman Empire. In the period of Turkish Republic, this tolerance doesn't decrease. Contrarily, it lasted increasingly. The Jews in Turkey left themselves to wide tolerance of the Turks. They were accepted from the time of Ottoman Empire till today by the Turks. They played an active role in every field. The Jews who were shown a large tolerance by after the Turks many difficulties in Europe, joint business life without hesitating; they played important roles in trade, in art and especially in state administration.[70]

The Jews didn't forget their taking refuge with Turkish protectorate and they said their gratitude in some ways. They celebrated the 400th anniversary of their repelling from Spain and taking refuge with Turkey in 1892. In messages edited and in poems written in that anniversary, they praised the Turks clearly and they expressed that they saw the Turks as a resquer. In one of poems. "If the Turk weren't be for us, when people were against us, they (nations except from the Turks, christions) would swallow us" it's evaluated as above.[71]

Tolerance towards the Jews lasted during the reign of Sultan Süleyman the Megnificant and in the

---

[70] For position of the Jews in the Ottoman state and tolerance of the Turks see; Ahmet Hikmet Eroğlu, *Osmanlı Devletinde Yahudiler*, Ankara 1997 p. 51-65.

period of Sultans. The Turks became again protector of the ones who were repelled from Portugal, France, Poland, Italy and Russia.[72] The Jews in Turkey, today founded wakfs to express tolerance and protectorate of the Turks towards the Jews. They elebrated the 500th anniversary of their taking shelter in Turkey and they made the world hear about Turkish zealousy. Naim Güleryüz, who is a Jew and deputy of 500th year wakf's head expressed this situation with these sentences: "in 1992, the purpose was not only to remember and celebrate an event occured 500 years ago but also to inform the world about a harmonious life, unity, universalism lasted over 500 years. It was also introduction of superior characteristics of the Turks as nation and state and that of Turks' humane approchement by two words as 'sample to humanity' to whole people. Some celebration activities such as symposiums, conference, concerts, exhibitions, publications and films have expressed the life of the Jews for over 500 years in the Ottoman Empire and Republic of Turkey. Also they display that it's possible to live in peace and harmany for people from different races and generations under one flag."[73]

[71] Abraham Galante, *Cinquiémé Recueil de Documents Concermants lel Juif de Turquie*, Istanbul, 1995, p. 5-8.

[72] A. Küçük, *ibid*, p. 102-112; Naim Güleryüz, "Türk Musevileri" *Musevilerle 500 yıl*, Publications of Turkish Ministry of Tourism, Ankara, 1992, p. 9-13.

[73] Naim Güleryüz, "Türk Musevilleri", *Musevilerle 500 yıl*, p. 8.

Conclution:

The Turks were friends of those who have fallen into adversity during their history; they considered everybody as a holy creature of Allah whatever their religion and race were and they tolerated them without any exception and they were used to administer justly.

Also today the Turks display all examples of tolerance both to the Jews and Christians under their domination. Religious minorities (the Armenians, the Greeks, the Bulgarians and the Jews) nor the muslim ones (like the Araps) did what they were supposed to do. They were supposed to help the Turks while the Turks were occupied with war and they were offented by all sides. However those minorities behaved on the contrary. Even some of them helped and collaborated with enemies of the Turks. Despite all these negations, the Turks didn't need for revenge, they kept their tolarence towards both muslim and non-muslim minorities. The Turks avoided from different treatment even towards the ones making activities against the unification of the Turkish state with it's country and nation. Even today, in spite of all these it's argued that important and high ranks are occupied by the people who hesitate from saying that "I'm Turkish!", clearly.[74]

[74] Mehmet Osmanoğlu, "Türkler ve Azınlıklar", *Yeni Hayat Dergisi*, Haziran 1995, p. 17-20.

The Armenians, the Greeks and the Jews are just example for religious tolerance of the Turkish nation. These examples can be varied and found in all parts of history. However, sometimes it's disputed whether this good intention and tolerance damaged the Turkish nation or not. A Turk is a symbol of good intention and sincetery, profit by pure and honorable feelings of the Turks "didn't improve" and won't improve.

Schaman, about to enter trance.